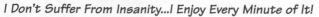

I Don't Suffer From Insanity...I Enjoy Every Minute of It!

Copyright © 2006 Barbara Johnson
Published by DaySpring® Cards, Inc.
Siloam Springs, Arkansas 72761
www.dayspring.com

Unless otherwise indicated, Scripture quotations are taken from
The Holy Bible, New International Version® NIV®. © 1973, 1978,
1984 by International Bible Society. Used by permission of Zondervan.

Other Scripture quotations are taken from: The New Century Version®
(NCV). Copyright © 1987, 1988, 1991 by Word Publishing, a division of
Thomas Nelson, Inc. Used by permission. All rights reserved. The Living Bible
(TLB) copyright © 1971 by permission of Tyndale House Publishers, Inc., Wheaton,
IL. The New King James Version (NKJV). Copyright © 1982 by Thomas Nelson, Inc.
Used by permission. All rights reserved. The New Revised Standard Version of the
Bible (NRSV), © 1989. Division of Christian Education, National Council of
Churches. Used by permission of Zondervan Publishing House, Licensee.
The NEW AMERICAN STANDARD BIBLE®
(NASB), © Copyright The Lockman Foundation
1960, 1962, 1963, 1968, 1971, 1972, 1973,
1975, 1977, 1995. Used by permission
(www.Lockman.org). The Holy Bible, King
James Version (KJV).

Printed in China
ISBN 1594495041

Let your light shine! Deliberately choose to look for joy in every step of your journey through life and to share it with others. When you do, you will be blessed with happiness no matter what your circumstances are.

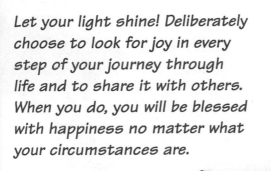

January 1

Remember: Each of us can decrease the suffering of the world by adding to its joy.

DAWNA MARKOVA

December 31

We _can_ do it. We _can_ sparkle with joy in the deepest, darkest basement, because the Lord is our battery pack that empowers us to smile and laugh no matter how dire our circumstances appear to be.

January 2

Emergency operator:
   911, what is your emergency?
Caller: Could you send the
   police to my house?
Emergency operator:
   What's wrong there?
Caller: I called and someone
   answered the phone,
   but I'm not there.

December 30

My mind contains many good ideas, but it's not always easy to squeeze one out.

Ashleigh Brilliant

January 3

It's no use having a good memory, unless you have something good to remember.

ASHLEIGH BRILLIANT

December 29

Mothers seem to have a sixth sense about impending disasters. It's as if we have a built-in radar system attached to an invisible satellite dish that constantly whirls on top of our heads, anxiously searching for any hint of trouble. Otherwise why would the classic warnings come so easily to us?

January 4

There is nothing in your life that God and you cannot handle together— if you get out of the way and let Him be in control. He can turn your troubles into blessings, and then He can use those blessings to add depth to your spirit so that your praise for Him is even more fervent and joyous and your life is an inspiration to others.

December 28

*Stop asking Why? and instead
hold fast to God's promises.
God...always does exactly what he says.*

2 CORINTHIANS 1:19 TLB

January 5

In God's economy, nothing is wasted—not one flicker of hope, not a single act of kindness, not one imponderable "Why?" And in the darkest pit of despair, when God gives us the light to take only one step at a time, His message to us is still simply: Trust Me.

January 6

Give of yourself; offer your services to a hospital or church. Help people. The law of giving will reward you tenfold.

ALFRED A. MONTAPERT

January 7

Jesus was content to be born
in a stable so that we may have
a mansion when we die.

Though he was rich...
he became poor, so that
you through his poverty
might become rich.

2 CORINTHIANS 8:9

December 25

Two ninety-year-old men, Herb and Herman, were at the funeral service for another ninety-year-old pal. After the benediction, they lingered, looking at the open casket of the deceased brother. Finally Herb said to Herman, "You know, it's hardly worth going home."

January 8

One of the ways we share God's love is through encouragement. Someone said the word encourage means "to fill the heart, to puff it up, to enlarge it." By encouraging a friend, we give that person a special gift.

December 24

Mental floss regularly with
God's Word to avoid truth decay.

DARLYNE J. ERICKSON

January 9

When grief is intensified during the holidays, you may feel yourself dissolving into a whirlpool of helplessness. But remember: While pain is inevitable in this life, misery is optional! You still have a choice about how you respond to the pain that turns your world upside down.

December 23

The Lord your God is with you, he is mighty to save. He will take great delight in you, he will quiet you with his love, he will rejoice over you with singing.

ZEPHANIAH 3:17

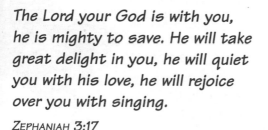

January 10

The youngest children enrolled in a church preschool always steal the show at the annual Christmas program. Last year the children—none of whom could yet read—held up brightly colored three-foot-high placards that spelled out Christmas words. The highlight came when one foursome walked onstage in reverse order and proudly spelled RATS.

December 22

Humor is the prelude to faith, and laughter is the beginning of prayer.

REINHOLD NIEBUHR

January 11

Remember, every cloud has a silver lining...and sometimes a bolt of lightning.

December 21

Reaching out to others doesn't mean we adopt all their problems as our own.... Sometimes we can help others through the smallest—or silliest—acts of kindness.

December 20

Life is like riding a bicycle.
You don't fall off unless
you stop pedaling.

January 13

It's not the pace of life that concerns me, it's the sudden stop at the end.

December 19

This is a test. It is only a test.
If this were your actual life,
you would be given better instructions.

MYRNA NEIMS

January 14

Instead of criticizing yourself when you do something goofy, find a way to laugh about it.

The cheerful heart has a continual feast.

PROVERBS 15:15

January 15

SIGN POSTED ON GROCERY-STORE
BULLETIN BOARD:

For Sale:
Complete Encyclopedia Britannica.
Excellent condition.
No longer needed.
Wife knows everything.

January 16

One of the scariest things some [men] do is accompany their wives to the mall, especially at Christmastime, when the traffic is hectic and the stores are packed. One researcher said the stress levels in some men skyrocket when they're faced with crowded stores.

David Lewis

December 15

For Christians, home is heaven!
That's our eternal home as well as
our enduring hope, a hope someone
defined as He

Offers
Peace
Eternal.

January 18

Age is mostly a
matter of mind.
If you don't mind it,
it doesn't matter.

December 14

God believes in me,
so my situation is never hopeless.
He walks beside me,
so I am never alone.
God is on my side,
so I can never lose.

January 19

It might be a good idea to ask ourselves how we develop our capacity to choose for joy. Maybe we could spend a moment at the end of each day and decide to remember that day—whatever may have happened—as a day to be grateful for. In so doing we increase our heart's capacity to choose joy.

HENRI NOUWEN

December 12

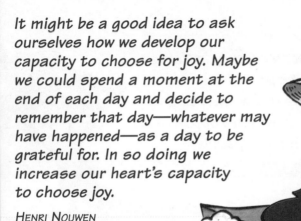

HAVE YOU HEARD ABOUT THE NEW BARBIE DOLLS?

Hot Flash Barbie: Press Barbie's bellybutton, and watch her face turn beet red while tiny drops of perspiration appear on her forehead. Comes with handheld fan and tiny tissues.

January 21

LITTLE KID'S INSTRUCTIONS ON LIFE:

- *When your dad is mad and asks you, "Do I look stupid?" don't answer him.*
- *Never try to baptize a cat.*
- *Never trust a dog to watch your food.*
- *Never tell your little brother that you're not going to do what your mom told you to do.*
- *Remember you're never too old to hold your father's hand.*

December 11

Youth looks ahead,
Old age looks back,
Middle age looks tired.

January 22

Be open-minded,
but not so open-minded that
your brains fall out.

December 10

PRICELESS GIFTS TO GIVE FOR FREE

The gift of a cheerful disposition: The easiest way to feel good is to extend a kind word to someone, even if it's just saying hello or thank you.

January 24

Sometimes my mind is so uncomfortable, I wish I could go somewhere and take it off.

ASHLEIGH BRILLIANT

December 8

Risk-takers' lives are enriched, not just by the joy we experience, but also by the tears we shed. Step out in faith and do what you feel led to do, whether it's something simple, like volunteering for a new outreach ministry with your church, or something more complicated— like applying for astronaut training!

December 7

A well-informed person...
is somebody who has the same
views and opinions as yours.

January 26

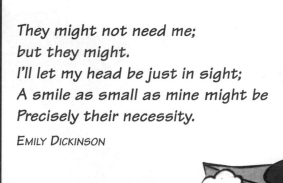

They might not need me;
but they might.
I'll let my head be just in sight;
A smile as small as mine might be
Precisely their necessity.

EMILY DICKINSON

January 27

The rooster may crow, but it's the hen who delivers the goods.

December 5

What could be better than knowing we're "leaning on the everlasting arms" of Jesus? What could be more encouraging than remembering that we're loved by the almighty One who created us—and died for us! What could be more rewarding than the knowledge that the Carpenter from Nazareth has built mansions for us in heaven!

January 28

Even when I am old and gray, do not forsake me, O God, till I declare your power to the next generation, your might to all who are to come.

PSALM 71:18

December 4

I've figured out why people get gray hair. It's from worrying about their teeth falling out!

January 29

How far you go in life depends on your being tender with the young, compassionate with the aged, sympathetic with the striving, and tolerant of the weak and the strong—because someday in life you will be all of these.

GEORGE WASHINGTON CARVER

December 3

It's tough to be at the age at which, when you go all out, you end up all in.

January 30

Middle age is when you choose
your cereal for the fiber,
not for the toy.

December 2

A little boy took his pet iguana to school to show the other kids. If you've ever seen an iguana, you know it has a large flap of skin, called the dewlap, that hangs down from the neck. The kids asked what it was, and when the boy explained, a little girl said, "Oh! My grandma has one of those."

January 31

God gave us memories so that we might have roses in December.

SIR JAMES M. BARRIE

December 1

The hope of heaven, the knowledge that we'll someday enjoy "peace eternal," means we can face <u>anything</u> here on earth as long as we focus on the joy that's waiting for us in heaven.

February 2

Oh, that I had the wings of a dove!
I would fly away and be at rest.

November 29

Inside every older person,
There's a younger person,
Wondering what happened.

ASHLEIGH BRILLIANT

February 3

Most people have minds like concrete: mixed up or permanently set.

JEFF ROVIN

November 28

For God has not given us a spirit of fear, but of power and of love and of a sound mind.

2 TIMOTHY 1:7 NKJV

February 4

I went to a bookstore and
asked the saleswoman,
"Where's the self-help section?"
She said if she told me,
it would defeat the purpose.

STEVEN WRIGHT

February 5

Menopause is a mother's revenge
for all the times you tried her
patience after age fifty.

ERMA BOMBECK

November 26

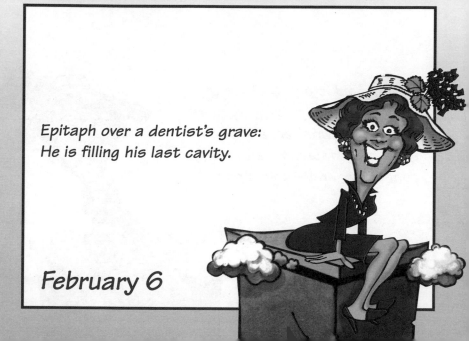

Epitaph over a dentist's grave:
He is filling his last cavity.

February 6

God is offering Himself to you daily, and the rate of exchange is fixed: your sins for His forgiveness, your hurt for His balm of healing, your sorrow for His joy. Give Him your pain. Give him the guilt you feel, the heartaches that come to us all. They are part of living, but if you focus on Jesus Christ, He alone can ease your heartache.

February 7

When one door closes, another door always opens—but those long hallways are a real drag.

PATTY WOOTEN

November 24

While a blessing of kindness
ripples outward to others,
it boomerangs right back to
the one who threw the pebble.

February 8

My philosophy is that we should just do our best—and laugh about the rest. We have to keep things in perspective.

November 23

My personal theory is that God designed parenthood, in part, as an enormous character-building exercise, and since God does not personally require character improvement, He didn't need to bother getting Adam to eat strained peas.

MEURER

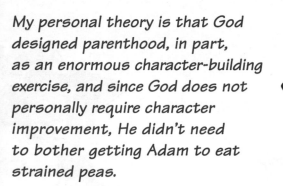

November 22

I'm looking forward to moving into that new body God has promised me in heaven. No more aches and pains, no more groans, no more corns or calluses. How wonderful to think of moving out of my earthly body.

February 10

Grandparent: A thing so simple, even a small child can operate it.

November 21

You know the only people who are <u>always</u> sure about the proper way to raise children? Those who've never had any.

BILL COSBY

February 11

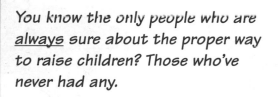

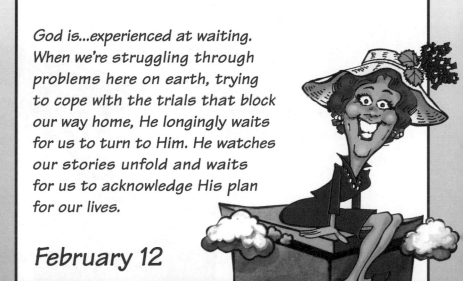

God is...experienced at waiting. When we're struggling through problems here on earth, trying to cope with the trials that block our way home, He longingly waits for us to turn to Him. He watches our stories unfold and waits for us to acknowledge His plan for our lives.

February 12

Wisdom doesn't necessarily come with age. Sometimes age just shows up all by itself.

TOM WILSON

November 19

You know it's time to throw in the towel when you'd fall apart completely if it weren't for static cling!

MARTIN A. RAGAWAY

February 13

One who is filled with joy preaches without preaching.

November 18

You are my hiding place; you will protect me from trouble and surround me with songs of deliverance. I will instruct you and teach you in the way you should go; I will counsel you and watch over you.

PSALM 32:7-8

February 14

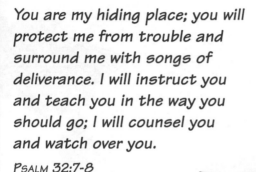

No matter how old she is, a mother watches her middle-aged kids for signs of improvement.

November 16

One of the greatest labor-saving inventions of today is tomorrow.

November 14

Heaven will be a spacious place, and all sorts of treasures will be available to us there. But the entryway is too small for a moving van; we can't take anything with us to paradise except the love we carry inside our hearts.

February 18

If God seriously plans to help with my problems...He has a busy day ahead of Him!

ASHLEIGH BRILLIANT

November 13

Middle age is when you want to see how long your car will last... instead of how fast it will go.

February 19

Erma Bombeck said when she went to sign up for an exercise class, they told her to wear loose clothing. "I said, 'Are you kidding? If I had any loose clothing I wouldn't need to take the class!'"

November 12

People with a heart for God
have a heart for people.

November 11

There are so many ways we can follow Jesus' example and be a servant to others. Sometimes we provide a gift of encouragement simply by doing ordinary work with cheerfulness.

February 21

Men are like parking spaces.
All the good ones are
already taken.

November 10

PRICELESS GIFTS TO GIVE FOR FREE

The gift of laughter: Share articles, funny stories, and cartoons to tell someone, "I love to laugh with you."

February 22

Let's resolve to be angels of joy and missionaries of mirth wherever we go today—and every day!

November 9

Instead of wearing the galoshes of gloom we need to wrap ourselves in the "garment of praise".

Give them beauty for ashes,
The oil of joy for mourning,
The garment of praise for
the spirit of heaviness.

ISAIAH 61:3 NKJV

February 23

You know you're getting older when...
"Happy Hour" is a nap!

November 8

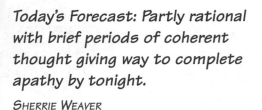

Today's Forecast: Partly rational with brief periods of coherent thought giving way to complete apathy by tonight.

SHERRIE WEAVER

February 24

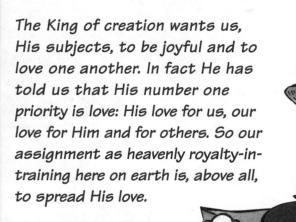

The King of creation wants us, His subjects, to be joyful and to love one another. In fact He has told us that His number one priority is love: His love for us, our love for Him and for others. So our assignment as heavenly royalty-in-training here on earth is, above all, to spread His love.

November 7

Sometimes it's an effort to receive God's forgiveness. We have to make a conscious decision to accept Christ's cleansing as a wonderful, expensive, sacrificial gift.

February 25

Jesus knows how you feel—hurt, scared, alone—and He's always with you to wrap you in His comfort blanket of love.

I am with you and will watch over you wherever you go.

GENESIS 28:15

November 6

ANOTHER TITLE DESTINED
TO BE A BESTSELLER:

Kids Are from Mars.
Parents Are from Cleveland.

TOM ARMSTRONG

February 26

One of the most comforting things for hurting parents is discovering there are hundreds of other parents out there who have gone through the same painful struggles—and survived.

November 5

Today is the tomorrow you worried about yesterday—but not nearly enough.

November 4

BUMPER STICKER:

When you do a good deed, get a receipt—in case heaven is like the IRS.

February 28

Author and pastor Max Lucado says he used to be a "closet slob" with the attitude, "Life is too short to match your socks; just buy longer pants!" Then...he got married!

November 3

Never ask old people how they
are if you have anything else
to do that day.

JOE RESTIVO

November 2

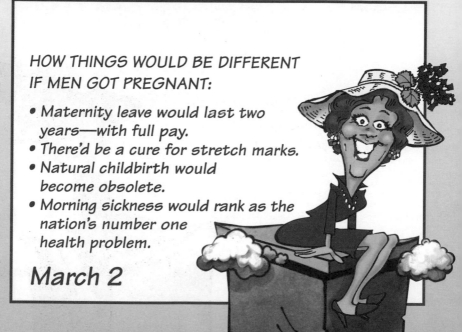

In the trials we've faced,
something good has happened too:
God has fine-tuned us so we are
more compassionate, more caring,
more loving, more aware of
others' pain.

March 3

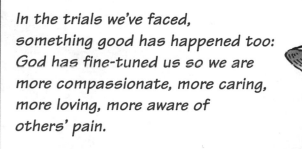

Healing comes when you realize
the light at the end of the tunnel
is not a train.

October 30

Kids are like sponges. They absorb all your strength and leave you limp. Give 'em a squeeze, and you get it all back.

October 29

To reach out to others,
we can start by sharing a smile,
an encouraging word,
an opportunity to laugh.

March 5

One of the side benefits of forgetting names and faces: You keep meeting new people every day!

E. FISCHER AND J. T. NOLAND

October 28

Insomuch as anyone pushes you nearer to God, he or she is your friend.

October 27

People who need to get older
* are much luckier*
Than people who need to get younger!

ASHLEIGH BRILLIANT

March 7

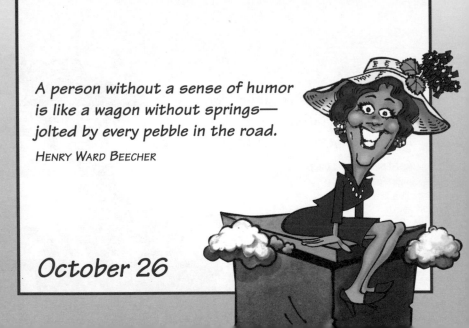

A person without a sense of humor is like a wagon without springs—jolted by every pebble in the road.

HENRY WARD BEECHER

October 26

How is it that you can gain two pounds by eating half a pound of fudge?

H. JACKSON BROWN JR.

March 8

OVERHEARD:

When I married my Mr. Right,
I didn't know his first name
was ALWAYS!

March 9

Lord Jesus Christ,
You are the journey,
the journey's end,
the journey's beginning.

DEAN MAYNE

October 24

For he will command his angels concerning you to guard you in all your ways.

PSALM 91:11

March 10

*Sometimes God calms the storm,
and sometimes He lets the storm
rage and calms His child.*

JEAN VAN DYKE

*Blessed are those...who walk in the
light of your presence, O Lord.*

PSALM 89:15

October 23

According to my birth certificate, I am living somewhere between estrogen and death, or, as someone said, between menopause and LARGE PRINT! But I don't have to act my age because, thank God, I've discovered a wonderful anti-aging remedy. In fact, it's been promoted since biblical times as a cure for a wide variety of problems. What is it? Laughter.

March 11

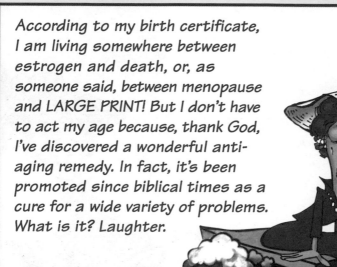

You're not old unless you get wrinkles in your heart!

October 22

Attitude is the mind's paintbrush.
It can color any situation.

March 12

We probably wouldn't worry about what people think of us if we could know how seldom they do.

BOB PHILLIPS

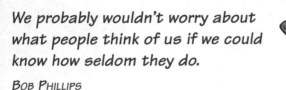

October 21

For attractive lips, speak words of kindness.
For lovely eyes, seek out the good in people.
For a slim figure, share your food
    with the hungry.
For beautiful hair, let a child run his
    fingers through it once a day.
For poise, walk with the knowledge
    that you'll never walk alone.

SAM LEVENSON

March 13

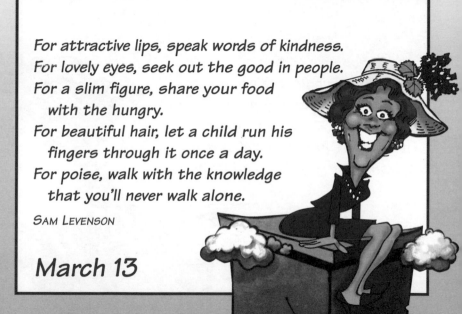

It's impossible to feel miserable
while imagining ourselves wearing
the crown Jesus has promised us
and saying, "Thank You, God!"
It's just as hard to stick a perky
geranium in your hat and be gloomy.

October 20

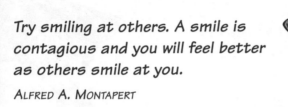

Try smiling at others. A smile is contagious and you will feel better as others smile at you.

ALFRED A. MONTAPERT

October 19

GOOD NEWS:
I've finally discovered the
Fountain of Youth.

BAD NEWS:
At my age, I've forgotten
what I wanted to do with it.

MARTIN A. RAGAWAY

March 15

The beautiful words of Ecclesiastes teach us there is "a time to get, and a time to lose; a time to keep, and a time to cast away." There are occasions in life when we must hang on—grip the hand of God tight and struggle fiercely to hold on to His promises. And then at the end of our lives, there is a time to let go of the struggles and simply fall into those everlasting arms of the Father.

March 16

The best vitamin for
making friends: B1.

October 17

Life is an adventure.
Hang on to your hat and
scream for all you're worth.

March 17

The idea that angels are real, that they intercede in our world to minister to God's children (that's us!), should inspire us to do a little angel-work ourselves whenever the opportunity arises.

October 16

As I love and encourage others...
as I lift up Jesus,
I serve Jesus,
I imitate Jesus,
I, too, am blessed.

March 18

Talking is sharing,
But listening is caring.

October 15

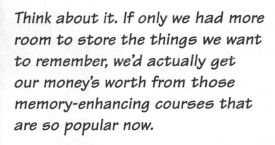

Think about it. If only we had more room to store the things we want to remember, we'd actually get our money's worth from those memory-enhancing courses that are so popular now.

March 19

Only two things are necessary to keep one's wife happy. One is to let her think she is having her own way. The other is to let her have it.

LYNDON B. JOHNSON

March 20

What a comforting thought—to imagine our grandchildren facing some tough decision someday or feeling lonely in some far-off place and suddenly remembering a grandmother's love—and being comforted by it.

October 13

Lewis and Clark were not really meant to explore the West for all those months. They simply did not want to admit (especially in front of Sacajawea) that they were lost.

SHERRIE WEAVER

March 21

*I am still confident of this: I will
see the goodness of the Lord in
the land of the living. Wait for the
Lord; be strong and take heart
and wait for the Lord.*

PSALM 27:13-14

October 12

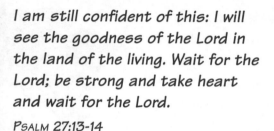

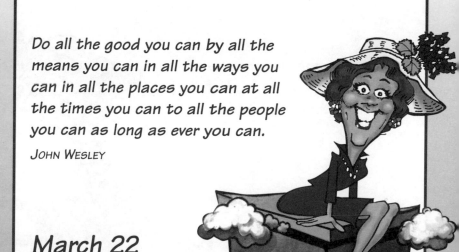

Do all the good you can by all the means you can in all the ways you can in all the places you can at all the times you can to all the people you can as long as ever you can.

JOHN WESLEY

March 22

The reason most people change their minds so often is that they never find one worth keeping.

JEFF ROVIN

October 11

We need four hugs a day for
survival. We need eight hugs a day
for maintenance. We need twelve
hugs a day for growth.

VIRGINIA SATIR

March 24

*We do God's work because
God promises to work in us
and through us.*

October 9

May the God of hope fill you with all joy and peace as you trust in him, so that you may overflow with hope by the power of the Holy Spirit.

ROMANS 15:13

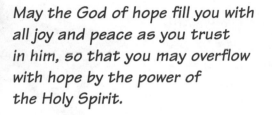

March 25

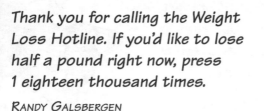

Thank you for calling the Weight
Loss Hotline. If you'd like to lose
half a pound right now, press
1 eighteen thousand times.

RANDY GALSBERGEN

October 8

Morning memory jog, upon arising:
It's gotten so I have to put a sign
beside my bed: "First the pants,
then the shoes!"

March 26

The worthiest cause is kindness, and it is timeless.

October 7

PRICELESS GIFTS TO GIVE FOR FREE

The gift of affection: Be generous with appropriate hugs, kisses, pats on the back, and handholds. Let these small actions demonstrate the love you have for family and friends.

March 27

Extra love from grandparents goes into a child's psychological bank account, which draws interest and can be used for an emotionally rainy day.

October 6

When Christ shall come
    with shout of acclamation
And take me home,
    what joy shall fill my heart!
Then I shall bow
    in humble adoration
And there proclaim,
    my God, how great Thou art!

STUART K. HINE

March 28

Whatever you and your house are like—whether your housekeeping system is the casual stow-and-slam method or the super-organized home where even the dustballs line up evenly under the bed, the most important thing to fill your home with is joy. What a blessing to step inside a home and immediately feel surrounded by a bubble of laughter and a blanket of love.

October 5

Warning! Humor may be hazardous to your depression.

The joy of the Lord is your strength.

NEHEMIAH 8:10

March 29

Beauty is only skin deep...
but fortunately,
I have very deep skin.

ASHLEIGH BRILLIANT

October 4

Blessed are they who have nothing to say and who cannot be persuaded to say it.

JAMES RUSSELL LOWELL

March 30

There are a lot of things that can make you feel old, and looking into the mirror (if you're wearing your glasses and the _wrong_ attitude) is one of them.

October 3

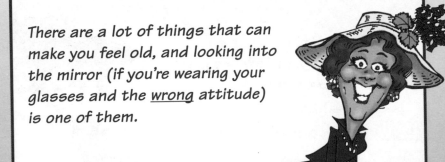

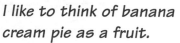

I like to think of banana cream pie as a fruit.

March 31

Trials are inevitable and we should consider them "pure joy" because the testing of our faith "develops perseverance" (JAMES 1:2-3 PARAPHRASED).

October 2

Have you given someone your smile?
Have you shared your laughter?
How about a hug?

DONNA WATSON

April 1

Music has provided soothing comfort. In happy times, it has inspired me to even higher realms of joy. In times of loneliness, it has brought abundant comfort. Truly, it is a gift of heaven on earth!

October 1

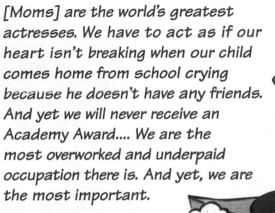

[Moms] are the world's greatest actresses. We have to act as if our heart isn't breaking when our child comes home from school crying because he doesn't have any friends. And yet we will never receive an Academy Award.... We are the most overworked and underpaid occupation there is. And yet, we are the most important.

MARY JO MALONE

April 2

A husband is a diplomat who remembers his wife's birthday but not her age.

JEFF ROVIN

September 30

In the midst of the darkness you will learn lessons you might never have learned in the day. We all have seen dreams turn to ashes—ugly things, hopeless experiences—but beauty for ashes is God's exchange. Offer yourself to God and ask for a spirit of praise so your whole being will be restored.

April 3

Many of us are in God's waiting room—and it seems we've been here forever. But you *do* meet such interesting people there—wonderful people who are also learning lessons as they suffer and grow. You are not alone; thousands like you are trying to find some relief from nights of loneliness.

September 29

You never can think what a good place Heaven is without knowing who [Jesus] was and what He did.

CHARLES DICKENS

April 5

A balanced diet is a
cookie in each hand.

Delight yourself in the Lord
and he will give you the
desires of your heart.

PSALM 37:4

September 27

HOW TO KNOW YOU'RE GETTING OLD:

You put your keys on the dresser, and they mysteriously wind up on top of the fridge. You lay the remote on the TV and find it later under the sofa. You slip your wallet into your purse, and the next morning it is on the front seat of your car.

April 6

Oh Lord, Bless the person who is too busy to worry in the daytime and too sleepy to worry at night.

CAROLINE SCHROEDER

September 26

Did you hear about the doorbell and hummingbird who fell in love? They had a little humdinger!

April 7

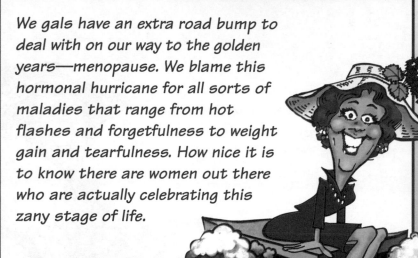

We gals have an extra road bump to deal with on our way to the golden years—menopause. We blame this hormonal hurricane for all sorts of maladies that range from hot flashes and forgetfulness to weight gain and tearfulness. How nice it is to know there are women out there who are actually celebrating this zany stage of life.

September 25

God cleanses us and makes us new. I like to say the one thing God cannot see is our sin because it is covered by the blood of Jesus. We are forgiven—and as Christians we know it!

April 8

Our lives seem to be controlled by whatever blow hits us next, sending us lurching from headache to heartache to horror story.
But we _can_ choose how we respond emotionally. We _can_ choose to hold on to the One who promises never to leave us.

September 24

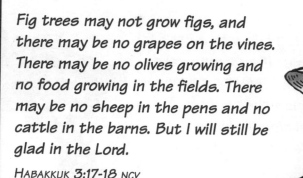

Fig trees may not grow figs, and there may be no grapes on the vines. There may be no olives growing and no food growing in the fields. There may be no sheep in the pens and no cattle in the barns. But I will still be glad in the Lord.

HABAKKUK 3:17-18 NCV

April 9

Even when the answers don't come, if we can vent our grief, healing oozes almost unnoticed into our lives.

I will never leave you nor forsake you.

JOSHUA 1:5

September 22

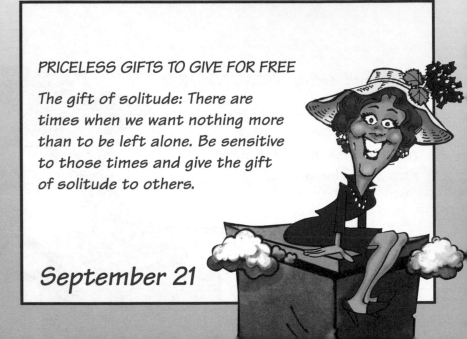

KITCHEN RULES

1. If a messy kitchen is a happy kitchen, my kitchen is delirious.
2. A husband is someone who takes out the trash and gives the impression he just cleaned the whole kitchen.
3. Countless people have eaten in this kitchen...and gone on to lead normal lives.

April 12

I can't cook, hate to clean, and loathe ironing. The only thing domestic about me is that I was born in this country.

PHYLLIS DILLER

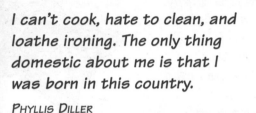

September 20

The happiest marriages are surely those where love and laughter overcome any brokenness. Between these couples, laughter is a natural part of every day.

April 13

*HAVE YOU HEARD ABOUT
THE NEW BARBIE DOLLS?*

*Post-Menopausal Barbie:
She wets her pants when
she sneezes, forgets where
she put things, and cries a lot.
Comes with micro-Depends
and Kleenex.*

September 19

Jesus' gift to us is eternal life, something we don't deserve, didn't work for, and can't buy for any price.

April 14

When we pray in His name,
God has promised to listen.
All we have to do is...do it!

September 18

Friends help us just by their willingness to laugh at the goofiness that unexpectedly pops into our lives to brighten the dark places.

April 15

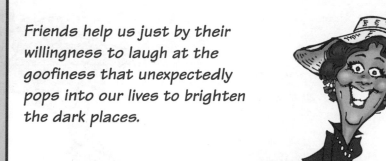

Two things every mom needs:
Velcro arms and a Teflon heart.

September 17

*THERE ARE THREE WAYS
TO GET SOMETHING DONE:*

* *Do it yourself.*
* *Hire someone to do it.*
* *Forbid your kids to do it.*

April 16

I've discovered an interesting phenomenon: If you keep microwaving bacon until it gets "real crispy" it will eventually melt down, and you will have to suck the flavor out of the paper towel.

September 15

Signs you're getting old:
Dialing long distance wears you out.

September 14

Truly, memory is a mental bank account. In it we deposit the treasures of our lives so that, in time of need, we can withdraw hope and courage. These treasures are memories large and small: splashes of joy ranging from a pat on the back, the beauty of a full moon on a special evening, finding an empty parking space when we were in a terrible rush, enjoying a glorious sunset with someone we love.

September 13

More times than I can recount,
I know I have "received that
I might give"; I've been blessed
to be a blessing.

April 20

*Have you been there for someone
  who was hurting?
Did you go out of your way
  just to be kind?
Were you willing to share
  your time and your life?*

DONNA WATSON

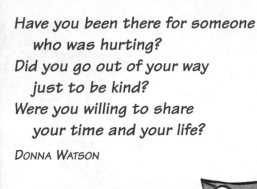

September 12

THEME SONGS FOR
BIBLICAL CHARACTERS

Noah: "Raindrops Keep
    Falling on My Head"
Adam and Eve: "Strangers in Paradise"
Moses: "There's a Place for Us"
Job: "I've Got a Right to Sing the Blues"

April 21

Sometimes I'm tempted to adapt a line I see every day on my car and transpose it onto the full-length mirror in my bedroom. It would say: Images in mirror are smaller than they appear.

September 11

Some women fight old age until the day they die. Lady Nancy Astor said, "I refuse to admit I am more than fifty-two, even if it does make my sons illegitimate."

April 22

The best way to forget all your troubles is to wear tight shoes.

September 10

Once you pass forty, your
"big break" will probably be a bone.

April 23

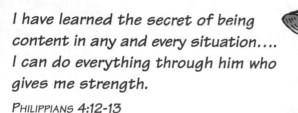

I have learned the secret of being content in any and every situation.... I can do everything through him who gives me strength.

PHILIPPIANS 4:12-13

April 24

I need some of my problems to help take my mind off some of the others.

ASHLEIGH BRILLIANT

September 8

Whether you're reminded to pray by the beeping of a digital watch or by the sound of the phone ringing in the wee hours of the morning...prayer helps.

April 26

BUMPER STICKER:

If you can't laugh at yourself...
I'll be glad to do it for you.

September 6

A LITTLE GIRL'S ESSAY ON PARENTS:

The trouble with parents is that they are so old when we get them, it's hard to change their habits.

April 27

What kind of perspective do you bring to unpleasant situations? Do you add to the gloom or introduce joy? Do you join in the grumbling or find something to laugh about? Do you follow our Lord's example and lift the spirits of "those bent beneath their loads"?

The Lord lifts the fallen and those bent beneath their loads.

PSALM 145:14 TLB

September 5

I know a little suffering is good for the soul, but somebody must be trying to make a saint out of me.

April 28

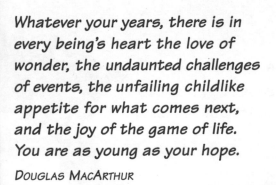

Whatever your years, there is in every being's heart the love of wonder, the undaunted challenges of events, the unfailing childlike appetite for what comes next, and the joy of the game of life. You are as young as your hope.

DOUGLAS MACARTHUR

September 4

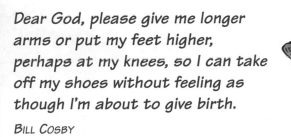

Dear God, please give me longer arms or put my feet higher, perhaps at my knees, so I can take off my shoes without feeling as though I'm about to give birth.

BILL COSBY

April 29

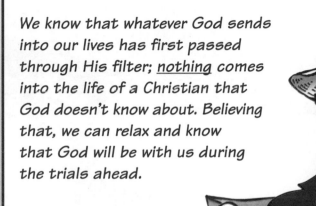

We know that whatever God sends into our lives has first passed through His filter; <u>nothing</u> comes into the life of a Christian that God doesn't know about. Believing that, we can relax and know that God will be with us during the trials ahead.

April 30

Learn to look for joy everywhere you go. When your many troubles are giving you a giant headache remember that the iron crown of suffering precedes the golden crown of glory—that's what we'll wear on that glorious day when we'll be in heaven jumping for joy with our heavenly Father!

May 1

Singing lifts our spirits. It's just plain good for us. Whether we sing with trained voices that bring thundering applause or off-key screeching, by the time our songs of praise reach heaven they're all equally beautiful.

September 1

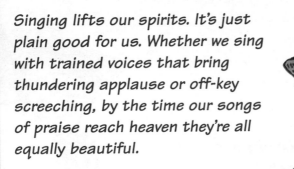

Marriage is taking on another person in life. It is not usually planned from the beginning; you don't know who it will be when you are born...but somehow the two joined become one, even if it doesn't seem likely or at all possible.

CHARIS COLLINS

May 3

A man had just undergone surgery, and as he came out of the anesthesia, he said, "Why are all the blinds drawn, Doctor?" "There's a big fire across the street, and we didn't want you to wake up and think the operation was a failure."

August 30

If you laugh a lot, when you get older, your wrinkles will be in the right places.

ANDREW MASON

Praise the Lord, O my soul, and forget not all his benefits.

PSALM 103:2

May 4

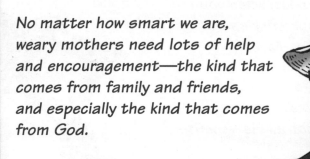

No matter how smart we are, weary mothers need lots of help and encouragement—the kind that comes from family and friends, and especially the kind that comes from God.

August 29

Life isn't always what we want,
but it's what we've got. So, with
God's help, choose to be joyful.

May 5

Sometimes we feel like we're smothering under the weight of all our problems, then someone comes along and fluffs us up with a word of encouragement.

August 28

MORE TRUTHS BROUGHT
TO US BY CHILDREN:

- Don't let your mom brush your hair when she's mad at your dad.
- If your sister hits you, don't hit her back. It's always the second person who gets caught.

May 6

Veni, vedi, visa

Translation: I came, I saw, I did a little shopping.

August 27

When something is restored it pops back in place, like an out-of-joint bone that is popped back into alignment, relieving the pain. Encouragement works like an emotional chiropractor—and both "doctor" and patient benefit from the treatment. As someone said, "Encouragement is a double blessing. Both giver and receiver are blessed."

May 7

How is it that one careless match can start a forest fire, but it takes a whole box to start a campfire?

May 8

The church is supposed to be a hospital for sinners, not a hotel for saints.

August 25

THINGS TO DO TODAY:

• Get up
• Survive
• Go to bed.

COREY J. ROSE

May 9

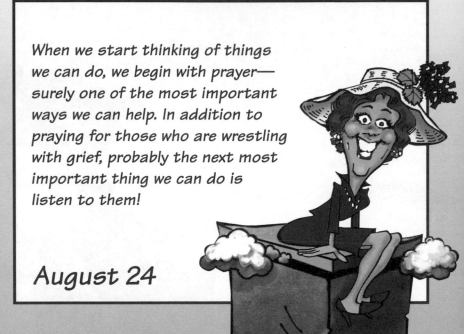

When we start thinking of things we can do, we begin with prayer—surely one of the most important ways we can help. In addition to praying for those who are wrestling with grief, probably the next most important thing we can do is listen to them!

August 24

IMPONDERABLES FROM
THE GAME OF LIFE:

• Why are there interstate
  highways in Hawaii?
• Why do we drive on parkways
  and park on driveways?

May 10

Put on tender mercies, kindness,
humility, meekness, longsuffering;
bearing with one another, and
forgiving one another....
But above all these things
put on love.

COLOSSIANS 3:12-14 NKJV

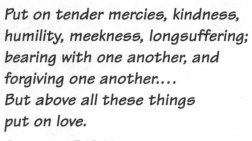

August 23

God loves me so much that
He will accept me just as I am...
But He loves me too much to
leave me that way!

May 11

To love and be loved is to feel the sun from both sides.

May 12

The only good thing about the decline of my memory is that it has brought me closer to my mother, for she and I now forget everything at the same time.

BILL COSBY

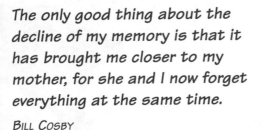

August 21

In order to realize the worth of the anchor, we need to feel the stress of the storm.

CORRIE TEN BOOM

May 13

I would rather walk with God in
the dark than go alone in the light.

MARY GARDINER BRAINARD

August 20

The glory of each morning is that it offers us a chance to begin again.

The steadfast love of the Lord never ceases, his mercies never come to an end; they are new every morning; great is your faithfulness.

LAMENTATIONS 3:22-23 NRSV

May 14

In good times and bad, music has always been a part of my life flowing through the laughter as well as the trials. To me, it is a gift from God— a bit of heaven He loans to us while we live on earth to help us survive the hard times, to celebrate the good times, and especially to praise Him in a way no other method can match.

August 19

*HAVE YOU HEARD ABOUT
THE NEW BARBIE DOLLS?*

*No-More-Wrinkles Barbie:
Erase those pesky crow's-feet and
lip lines with a tube of Skin Sparkle-
Spackle from Barbie's own line of
exclusive age-blasting cosmetics.*

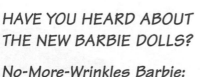

May 15

She who laughs last thinks the slowest.

August 18

Pain *is* inevitable. We can't prevent it, and sometimes we can't stop it once it's started. But we can *choose* not to be miserable. Invite Jesus to come into your fiery furnace with you, and He will place His loving hands under you and lift you up into His strong arms of protection.

May 16

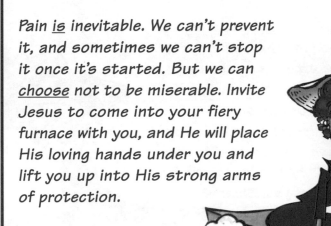

Beauty Tip: Beware of tucking your dress into the back of your underwear after using the rest room. You'll know this personal grooming error has occurred when you hear snickers from the people you pass on the street. Another giveaway will be the draft you feel on the back of your thighs.

August 17

In your grief, go limp,
And let others carry you for a while.
In doing so, you'll make a friend!

May 17

Amazing! If you hang something in a closet for a while, it shrinks two sizes.

August 16

While we're not really sure where heaven is, the Bible often refers to it as being up or above. That produces one of the "side effects" of heavenly thinking. When we're focusing on the joy we'll know in heaven, our thoughts turn heavenward—that's upward. Our hopes rise, and life down here is more bearable.

May 18

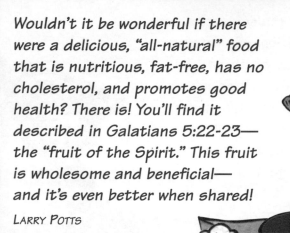

Wouldn't it be wonderful if there were a delicious, "all-natural" food that is nutritious, fat-free, has no cholesterol, and promotes good health? There is! You'll find it described in Galatians 5:22-23—the "fruit of the Spirit." This fruit is wholesome and beneficial—and it's even better when shared!

LARRY POTTS

August 15

This bumper sticker was punctuated with a bold cross: No matter which direction I'm heading, I'm homeward bound!

August 14

The trouble with doing something right the first time is that nobody appreciates how difficult it was.

May 20

Then you will call out, and the Lord will answer. You will cry out, and he will say, "Here I am."

ISAIAH 58:9 NCV

August 13

Give a friend a phone call or write a letter. Let that person know he or she is in your thoughts and prayers. Offer a word of encouragement—the oxygen to the soul.

ALFRED A. MONTAPERT

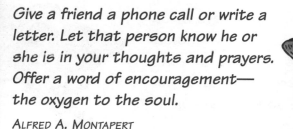

May 21

When we're thinking of ways we can follow Jesus' example and show a servant's heart to those in need, there's no better gift we can give them than the hope of heaven!

August 12

Being tickled to death is a great way to live. Jumping for joy is good exercise.

May 22

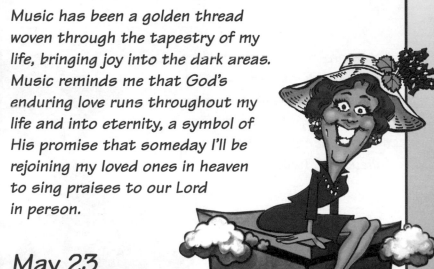

Music has been a golden thread woven through the tapestry of my life, bringing joy into the dark areas. Music reminds me that God's enduring love runs throughout my life and into eternity, a symbol of His promise that someday I'll be rejoining my loved ones in heaven to sing praises to our Lord in person.

May 23

There are several things that may cause men's stress levels to rise. One stressful activity is brushing their hair and finding that they're becoming, shall we say, folicularly challenged.

August 10

Someone has equated laughter with changing a baby's diaper. "It doesn't change things permanently, but it makes everything OK for a while."

May 24

The second day of a diet is
always easier than the first.
By the second day you're off it.

August 9

Have you paid someone
a compliment lately?
Have you told a friend
how special he or she is?
Have you listened with your
eyes and your ears?

DONNA WATSON

May 25

Prayer is asking for rain.
Faith is carrying an umbrella.

August 8

Remember, you may be older today than you have ever been before, but you are younger than you will ever be again!

May 26

Life becomes much easier, once you get through youth, middle age, and old age.

ASHLEIGH BRILLIANT

August 7

It doesn't take great wisdom to energize a person, but it does take sixty seconds. That's the amount of time it takes to walk over and gently hold someone we love.

GARY SMALLEY AND JOHN TRENT

May 27

Grandma Brown took her two grandchildren to the zoo.... They stopped before a huge cage of storks. Grandma told the two youngsters that these were the birds that brought both of them to their dad and mom. The two children looked at one another, then the oldest leaned over and whispered in his sibling's ear, "Don't you think we ought to tell Grandma the truth?"

JAMES E. MYERS

May 28

God grant me the senility to forget the people I never liked anyway, the good fortune to run into the ones I do—and the eyesight to know the difference.

August 5

As far as the east is from the west, so far has He removed our transgressions from us.

PSALM 103:12 NASB

Now, if God would just do that with our gray hair and wrinkles, we'd be in great shape!

NANCY L. JACKSHAW

May 29

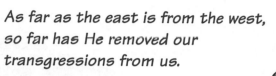

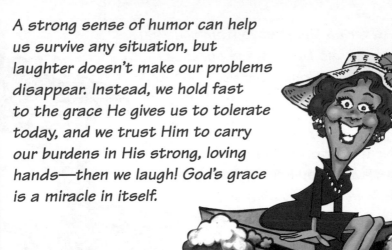

A strong sense of humor can help us survive any situation, but laughter doesn't make our problems disappear. Instead, we hold fast to the grace He gives us to tolerate today, and we trust Him to carry our burdens in His strong, loving hands—then we laugh! God's grace is a miracle in itself.

August 4

One of the best bonuses about being—or just _acting_—joyful is that inevitably the joy we share is reflected back to us just when we need it most.

May 30

Dear Lord, prop us up in all our leaning ways.

I will uphold you with my righteous right hand.

ISAIAH 41:10

August 3

There are two kinds of women who will pay big bucks for a makeup mirror that magnifies their faces. The first are young models who need to be sure to cover every eyelash and define their lips. The second group are women who, without their glasses, can't even find their faces.

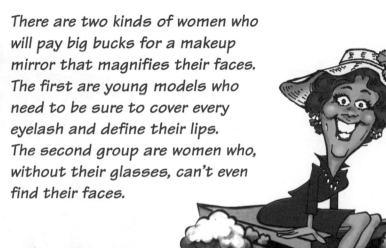

May 31

Tell a man there are four hundred billion stars, and he'll believe you. Tell him a bench has wet paint, and he has to touch it.

STEVEN WRIGHT

June 1

The blessings that come from reaching out to others cannot be overestimated.

June 2

Reminiscing helps us put our lives into perspective. As we get older, we can see how each stage, every memory, fits into the grander scheme of things. My life has included sorrow as well as happiness. And all those emotions, all those bittersweet memories have created what I like to think of as a bright, colorful, firmly woven tapestry.

July 31

I write down everything I want to remember. That way, instead of spending a lot of time trying to remember what it is I wrote down, I spend the time looking for the paper I wrote it down on.

PAT HANSEN

June 3

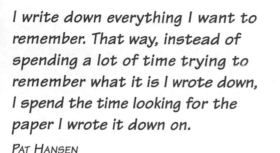

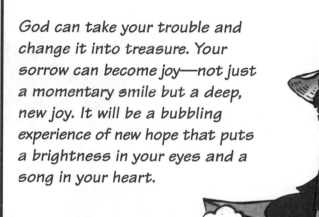

God can take your trouble and change it into treasure. Your sorrow can become joy—not just a momentary smile but a deep, new joy. It will be a bubbling experience of new hope that puts a brightness in your eyes and a song in your heart.

June 4

Thinking will get us to the foot of the mountain. Faith will get us to the top.

July 29

The great beautifier is a contented heart and a happy outlook.

June 5

I still don't know the answer to all the "whys" that have churned up my life, but I no longer need to know. Instead of questioning God, I've learned to search for ways God has used these experiences for good—to fine-tune us in our spiritual growth.

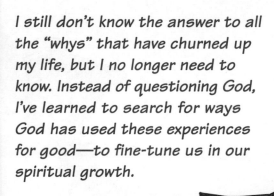

July 28

Under His wings, under His wings,
Who from His love can sever?
Under His wings my soul shall abide,
Safely abide forever.

W. O. CUSHING AND IRA D. SANKEY

June 6

Being a grandparent doesn't mean we're old. But it does mean we have a special opportunity. We can be a source of unfailing, unquestioning, nonjudgmental, nonstop, full-powered love for these children.

June 7

Our days are identical suitcases—all the same size—but some people can pack more into them than others.

BITS & PIECES

July 26

Those who hope in the Lord will renew their strength. They will soar on wings like eagles; they will run and not grow weary, they will walk and not be faint.

Isaiah 40:31

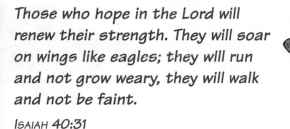

June 8

Instead of looking for answers to the unanswerable questions, look for joy in the life you've been given and:
Let yourself be glad you're alive.
Have genuine happiness despite your condition.
Enjoy laughter.
It's available everywhere once you start looking for it.

NORMA BARZMAN

July 25

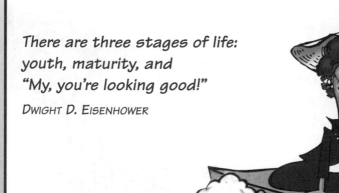

There are three stages of life: youth, maturity, and "My, you're looking good!"

DWIGHT D. EISENHOWER

June 9

Oh, no! Not another learning experience!

Continue in what you have learned and have become convinced of.

2 TIMOTHY 3:14

July 24

Even if you think you don't have a talent for happiness, act as if you do. You'll find that joy is like a vaccine that immunizes you against all sorts of maladies. Joy opens our hearts to see God's power at work in ourselves and in our world.

June 10

When we're able to relinquish
all our problems, all our worries,
and all our sins to the Lord,
we are free to live the guilt-free
lives He planned for us.

July 23

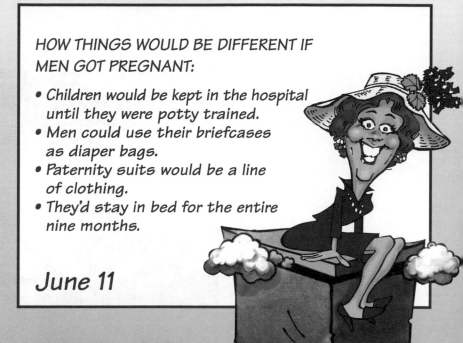

HOW THINGS WOULD BE DIFFERENT IF MEN GOT PREGNANT:

- Children would be kept in the hospital until they were potty trained.
- Men could use their briefcases as diaper bags.
- Paternity suits would be a line of clothing.
- They'd stay in bed for the entire nine months.

June 11

It is bad to suppress laughter. It goes back down and spreads to your hips.

FRED ALLEN

July 22

May God's joy shine down on you like the rays of the sun, filling your heart, soothing your spirit, and easing your pain. (But be sure to wear some kind of joy-screen; you wouldn't want to get overjoyed.)

June 12

SIGN POSTED ON HARRIED
SHOPKEEPER'S DOOR:

Out of my mind.
Be back in five minutes.

July 21

God often calls us to do things that we do not have the ability to do. Spiritual discernment is knowing if God calls you to do something, God empowers you to do it.

SUZANNE FARNHAM

July 20

Somewhere I read that for every single thing that goes wrong in our lives, we have fifty to one hundred blessings. What we need to do is learn to identify those blessings and spend more time counting—and being thankful for them!

June 14

Hope is the feeling you have that the feeling you have isn't permanent.

July 19

PRICELESS GIFTS TO GIVE FOR FREE

The gift of listening:
No interrupting, no daydreaming,
no planning your responses.
Just listen.

June 15

A woman marries a man expecting
he will change, but he doesn't.
A man marries a woman expecting
that she won't change, and she does.

June 16

When you find yourself caught in a web of unanswerable "whys," imagine your problems as a convoluted mass of yarn with such tangles that you could never straighten it out. Then imagine yourself dropping the tangles of your life into God's hands and leaving them there, knowing God alone can untangle the threads of our lives.

July 15

Just imagine living where love fills our lives so completely there won't be any empty spaces left in us to fill. Therefore we won't want anything. We'll be perfectly content—supremely satisfied. And since that will surely be the case, it seems quite likely that our heavenly palaces won't need to be very big because we won't have any stuff to store.

June 19

Behold, thou desirest truth in the inward parts: and in the hidden part thou shalt make me to know wisdom.

PSALM 51:6 KJV

July 14

For a thousand years in thy sight are but as yesterday when it is past, and as a watch in the night.

PSALM 90:4 KJV

June 20

God can help you find the <u>sonshine</u> inside yourself so you can laugh again. No matter where you are, He is with you.

July 13

Can it be an accident that "stressed" is "desserts" spelled backwards?

SUSAN MITCHELL

June 21

Just as one little pinch of salt can make all the difference in cooking, the light of one joyful Christian can radiate the love of Almighty God to the world.

July 12

Remember that when God created you, He gave you your emotions. He gave you tears to help drain off the abscess of pain that's broken your heart. And when you cry, remember that you're in good company. After all, Jesus wept, too, when His heart was broken.

June 22

One of my favorite ways to encourage others is by writing a quick note. Usually I jot something down on a silly cartoon I've seen somewhere. The message doesn't have to be long. Brief and sincere notes can uplift the receiver as much as a bouquet of flowers.

July 11

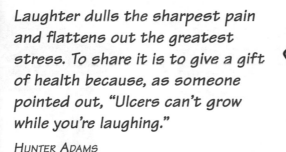

Laughter dulls the sharpest pain and flattens out the greatest stress. To share it is to give a gift of health because, as someone pointed out, "Ulcers can't grow while you're laughing."

HUNTER ADAMS

June 23

A woman taught the tiny tots in her Sunday school class to sing her favorite hymn, "Oh, the Consecrated Cross I Bear." Then came the Sunday morning when a concerned mother questioned the teacher about the songs she was teaching the children. Her child told her she'd learned to sing, "Oh, the constipated, cross-eyed bear."

June 24

Age gracefully? I think not!
Age ferociously instead. Seize
everything valuable within reach.
Extend. Question. Give. The face
will follow. All the cosmetic
surgeons in the world could
never produce such a face.

June 25

Do you know the difference between joy and happiness? Happiness depends on what is happening around us. But true joy just bubbles up from inside and is constant regardless of our circumstances.

July 8

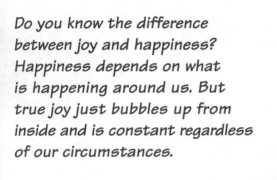

All we can take with us to heaven is what we leave behind in the lives we touch.

July 7

Happy moments—those moments when you feel fully alive—certainly exist. They swim by us every day like shining, silver fish waiting to be caught.

ALICE STEINBACK

June 27

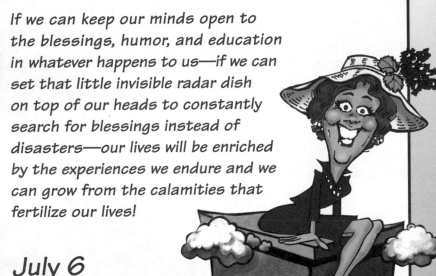

If we can keep our minds open to the blessings, humor, and education in whatever happens to us—if we can set that little invisible radar dish on top of our heads to constantly search for blessings instead of disasters—our lives will be enriched by the experiences we endure and we can grow from the calamities that fertilize our lives!

July 6

A little smile can brighten someone's day. And while you're smiling you might as well go one step further and share a chuckle or two.

June 28

*Life is an endless struggle, full
of frustrations and challenges.
But eventually you find a
hairstyle you like!*

June 29

Young at heart—slightly older in other places.

Satisfy us in our earliest youth with your lovingkindness, giving us constant joy to the end of our lives.

PSALM 90:14 TLB

July 4

It isn't easy being a mom, but prayer helps—and so does laughter. And sometimes it even helps to shed a cleansing tear or two. As someone said, tears are to the soul what soap is to the body.

July 3

Could we with ink the ocean fill
And were the skies of parchment made,
Were every stalk on earth a quill
And every man a scribe by trade
To write the love of God above
Would drain the ocean dry,
Nor could the scroll contain the whole
Tho' stretched from sky to sky.

FREDERICK M. LEHMAN

July 1

A word of encouragement at the right moment may be the turning point for a struggling life.

July 2